Hip Hop Twirls and Swirls!

By Sally Cowan

Reb and Mum went to
the Hip Hop Cup Show.

Reb hoped to win
first prize again!

Reb had on her black skirt
and her pink top.

And her best cap!

She brushed her pet rat, Rib.

The show began!

The first kid did a slow
arm wave.

He rolled his arms from left
to right and back again.

The next kid kicked his feet back and forth!

He twirled his arms.

It looked like he was rocking on a boat!

The third kid was a girl
in a green skirt.

Her name was Birdy.

Birdy ran on and did a glide.

She swirled her bright scarf.

Next, Birdy did a gull stomp!

Her feet went as quick
as a gull that stomps in the dirt!

Next, it was Reb.

First, she went to stir the pot!

She did a stir to the left,
and then a stir to the right!

Then, Reb did her robot step.

She flicked her arms
up and down and twirled from
side to side.

At the end, Reb crossed
her arms and looked out
with a cheeky smirk.

Rib swirled his tail!

Then, a big girl came out.

"The kids did some great
hip hop twirls and swirls!"
she said.
"But who will win?"

"Oh, it's **two** girls!"
said the big girl.

Reb and Birdy both came first!

"You were great!" said Reb.

"So were you!" said Birdy.

Then, both girls did a quick twirl and a high five!

CHECKING FOR MEANING

1. Where did Reb and Mum go? *(Literal)*

2. What was the name of the girl in the green skirt? *(Literal)*

3. Was it Reb's first time in the competition? How do you know? *(Inferential)*

EXTENDING VOCABULARY

forth	What does the word *forth* mean? How is it different from *fourth*?
stomp	What is a *gull stomp* in the text? When else might you use the word *stomp*?
smirk	How would you describe a *smirk*? What other word could have been used instead of *smirk* in the text?

MOVING BEYOND THE TEXT

1. Do you like dancing? Why or why not?

2. How would you describe hip hop dancing?

3. What do you think people like about hip hop?

4. What competition do you think you could come first in?

SPEED SOUNDS

ar	er	ir	ur	or

PRACTICE WORDS

first

skirt

twirled

girl

third

Birdy

swirled

dirt

twirls

smirk

stir

arm

swirls

girls

her

arms

forth

scarf

twirl

First